This book is from the library of:

The Heart of Prayer

Trish Yancey

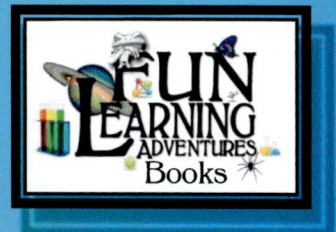

Fun Learning Adventures Books
Lake Worth, Florida

Library of Congress Cataloging-in-Publication Data

Yancey, Trish
    The Heart of Prayer

                                  2017906905

ISBN-13: 978-1-544-96093-7

Copyright © 2017 by Trish Yancey
First printing 2017 by Fun Learning Adventures, Lake Worth, Florida.

All rights reserved. Printed in the United States of America. No part of this publication may be reproduced or distributed in any form or by any means, or stored in a database or retrieval system, without the prior written permission of the publisher.

Visit us for permission at www.TrishYancey.com.

Infinite Love & Gratitude flows to ...

* Myrtle and Charles Fillmore, for opening to this paradigm shift in prayer, and birthing Unity.

* My incredible family for being exactly who you are, and for all your love and support. I am beyond blessed!

* The youth and High Watch Prayer Chaplains of Unity of the Palm Beaches, for bringing this from Heart to page.

* Mariah, Morgan, Julie, Emily, Gabriel, Zack and Tim for out-picturing this journey with me so beautifully ~ especially Tim, who made the pictures possible!

* To all who said yes when I asked, "Can I read this to you, and will you tell me what you think?" Tim, Steve, Shelli, Pat, Roger, Dave, Mariah, Julie, Emily, Morgan, Michele, Mark, Gavin, Antonio, Gabriel ... you are all among my greatest teachers!

* Reverend Taylor E. Stevens, my amazing mentor and valued friend, whose leadership and teachings truly birthed this endeavor ~ and whose unflagging patience and support continue to open my heart and eyes to the path ahead in new and glorious ways.

* The One Heart, Praying us all.

Before We Begin ...

What is prayer, and how do you pray? There are undoubtedly a multitude of unique answers to this question, but they all boil down to one; Prayer in its many forms is communion with the Ultimate Universal Creative Force or Law, which some choose to call God. The Unity Spiritual Movement was built on Prayer after its cofounder, Myrtle Fillmore, healed herself from terminal tuberculosis through the Power of Conscious, Affirmative Prayer. She was released from a lifetime of what her family described as inherited illness when she came to a new understanding of the incredible power within prayer. She Connected herself (and in time countless others) with the concept of Praying **through** our body, instead of **to** something outside of ourselves. This paradigm shift has the potential to alter the fabric of our reality as we commune with Divine Mind inside of us, instead of looking outward for something to change. Unity does not see God as a separate entity or "Super Being", rather as Source, Universal Law or Principle, or Divine Mind. This movement finds, as stated in Acts 17:28, "In God we live and move and have our being." We are a part of this Divine Field, and cannot be separated from it.

Unity's cofounder Charles Fillmore, referring to that Bible verse, expanded,

"God is in the universe as its constant 'breath' or inspiration; hence it is only necessary to find the point of contact in order to understand the One in whom we all 'live, and move, and have our being.'"

Myrtle Fillmore took the concept of our innate Divinity even further with her beliefs about prayer, which led to her healing. She made a life-altering assertion with her statement,

"Sometimes we pray to a God outside of ourselves. It is the God in the midst of us that frees and heals. With our eye of faith we must see God in our flesh, see that wholeness we are praying for in every part of the body temple. Prayers aren't sent out at all! Sometimes that is our trouble. Where would we send our prayers? We should direct them to our minds and hearts and affairs. We commune with God-Mind within our own consciousness."

This is the goal of Affirmative, Heart Centered Prayer. Instead of beseeching some outside force to make something happen, we realize that we are Truly a part of the totality of what God (as Universal Law, Source, Principle or Divine Mind) is, and we commune with that Divine nature indwelling as we Connect with our Heart in Prayer. We do not pray to change outer circumstances; we Pray to align with the Divine (Christ Consciousness) within. When we live from that awareness, we can truly change the quality of our life experience, and ultimately become the Change we wish to see in the world around us.

Please note: In the text of this book, you will see some (seemingly) inappropriately capitalized words within sentences. Any terms in this style refer to that word in its Divine/God/Source context, not its earthly or sense-consciousness appearance. For example, our heart is an organ inside our body; our Heart is that space inside of us where we connect with Divine Mind.

Maybe sometimes you wonder why it is that we pray,
And if you decide to, just what you should say.

But before we peel back all those 'What Prayer Is' layers,
You need to know first that your thoughts can be Prayers.

Not those mindless ones zipping right past every hour,
It's the thoughts we think over that grow and have Power.

See those can be Prayers because those can Create;
They can make our life hard, or perhaps make it great.

Whether it's 'good' or it's 'bad', the seventh time or the eighth,
When you're thinking things over it's like having faith.

The thoughts we hold on to become things we Believe.
They can show us the Truth, but could also deceive.

They may bring us much closer to the Divine that we Are,
Or might hurt us so deeply we're left with a scar.

If we know it or not, our thoughts become things,
They could dig us a hole, or can offer us wings.

Our thoughts shape our world like our hands can shape clay …
So what kind of thought prayers will you Pray today?

But enough about thoughts now, there won't be a quiz …
Let's take time to explore other things our prayer is.

Though people may pray in such different ways,
It's like God is the sun and our prayers are the rays.

Each unique beam of light is the sun's emanation,
Just as each living creature is God's incarnation.

Prayer is a way to connect with our Source,
Checking in for advice before charting our course.

Reaching into the Silence, we find our Divine,
Receiving our Guidance in life's Grand Design.

It's thanks for things finished, a word to begin,
Peace when we're worried, quiet time to check In.

We plug in when we feel our Connection is lost,
And untangle the knots when our wires get crossed.

Prayer is the Heartbeat within Life Divine,
It brings forth our Christ Light and helps it to Shine.

As natural as breathing, in motion unceasing,
We can inhale Connection, and exhale releasing.

Then Connected, on Purpose, we'll move through each day.
Life is a gift when we Consciously Pray!

This is the Prayer we are here to explore,
No matter what kind we have practiced before.

We're taking it deeper, going right to the Core,
Exactly what Heart Centered Prayer is there for.

It's all of the prayers we might say every day,
But when they come from our Heart they have **MUCH** more to Say!

So now you may wonder, "Well where should I start?"
The first thing to do is Connect with your Heart.

Let your body relax when you want to begin.
Don't worry about what's coming or things that have been.

Turn off the outside. If you will, close your eyes.
Bringing Focus Within lets your God-Self arise.

Imagine your Heart at the Core of your Being,
That's where Prayer begins and from where you'll be Seeing.

Just how do you move yourself into your Heart?
That's what the next pages are here to impart.

Gently send all your focus right into that Place.
Envision it opening ~ see inside Light and Grace.

Feel yourself enter, just move on Within,
There is nothing 'outside' now, it's God-Space you're in.

The idea's to stay there the whole time you Pray.
Feel you've left? Just go back. Now you know the way!

Your breathing, of course, is of equal importance;
It's best with your Heart and your Breath in concordance.

Send the air through your Heart-Space each time you inhale,
The effect is quite different with that small detail.

If you'd like you can pause before letting it out,
It can feel so divine sometimes choosing that route.

Then as you exhale, allow stress to release;
With each respiration feel God-Space increase.

Your Breath is the road your Prayer travels along,
It's the musical notes in your own Sacred Song.

Like a grand figure eight, curving out ~ looping back …
Your Prayer is the car, and your Breath is the track.

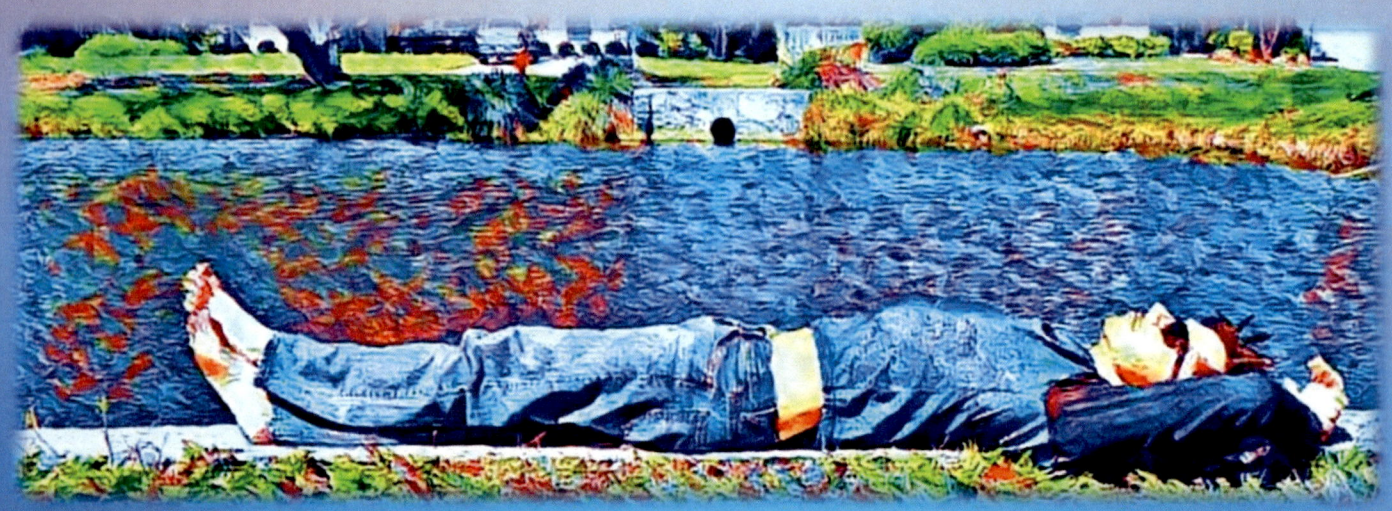

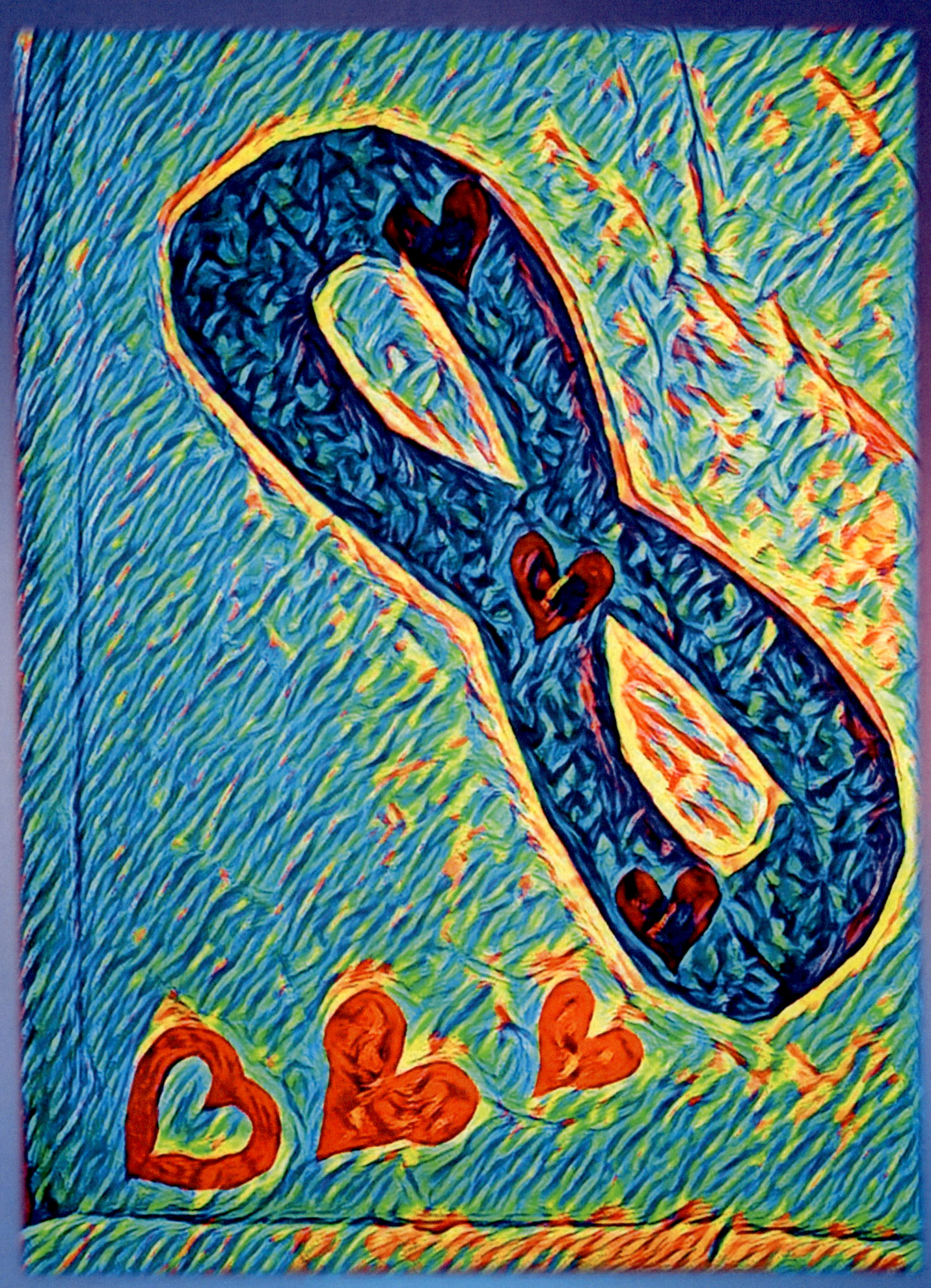

When you Pray by yourself, words just aren't really needed,
Your thoughts and your feelings can flow unimpeded.

From right where you're at simply Feel what you're feeling.
Your God-Self makes room for Release and for Healing.

Then Believe and have Faith, Affirming the Truth;
The Divine lives within you from old age to youth.

You will move through your Prayer surfing waves of sensation;
Relaxation ~ Connection ~ Affirmation ~ Celebration …
And then the energy shifts to **Creation**!

If your feelings bring words then just let them come through,
They may help you see things from a different view.

When you feel deep inside that your Prayer is Complete,
Express Thanks as you close ~ then as needed, repeat!

"But how could I lead someone else through a Prayer?"
You can totally do it! The same steps take you there.

Whether it's you and one other or a big giant group,
Link your chairs, feet or hands ~ form an Energy Loop.

Explain if you like why we join physically,
It shows we're all One in a way eyes can See.

No need to begin with "Dear God" or "Our Father",
You're **WITHIN** God already, you don't have to bother;

Just invite everyone into their Sacred Heart-Space,
Have them shift their attention gently right to that Place.

You'll ask them to Breathe in and out through their Heart,
One deep cleansing breath is a great way to start.

You know now at this point you're already Praying,
Any words that come out now, your God-Voice is Saying.

Remember, the words aren't the point of the Prayer,
The intent's to wake up the Connection that's there.

Whether you speak or stay silent, the goal is to **FEEL!**
THE FEELING IN PRAYER IS WHAT MAKES IT ALL REAL.

Once you've ridden that Prayer wave right through to the end,
You might close with, "and so it is", or maybe, "amen".

This is Affirmative, Heart Centered Prayer;
It's right there inside you each time, anywhere.

It's not asking for things or to just get your way,
It's letting the Voice of your Truth have its Say;

Remembering you are more than the body you're in,
Taking time in the Silence, stepping out of the din.

If you rest in the Silence, it's a whole new Creation,
Transforming from Prayer to become Meditation!

It doesn't need words, but it works with them too,
It's that Conscious Connection with Source inside you.

It's your Guidance, your Comfort, the Truth of your Being,
The Voice you will Hear on the path you'll be Seeing.

You can rely on it always to help see you through;
It's your whole Life's Creation right there inside you!

Any time you may need it, there's no need to wait …
Just **RELAX ~ CONNECT ~ AFFIRM ~ CELEBRATE** …

And then let your God-Self **CREATE**!

AFFIRMATIVE, HEART CENTERED PRAYER

RELAX
Your body and mind

CONNECT
Move your attention to your Heart,
open and Breathe through your Sacred Heart-Space,
connecting to your God-Self within

AFFIRM
Feel and declare your Faith and Belief in Truth

CELEBRATE
Feel and express Gratitude

CREATE!
Allow the Divine energy shift to go to work in your life
as your Prayer connection activates your Highest Good

Divine Discussions ... Quick Queries ...

Now that you've had a chance to read the book, let's chat!

* Do you pray? When? How? Why? Where?

* Have you ever prayed out loud with other people?
  How did you feel?

* What does "your thoughts can be Prayers" mean to you?

* What do you think the author meant when she said, "Our thoughts shape our world like our hands can shape clay"?

* Some words in the middle of sentences are capitalized. Why do you think that is?

* What do you feel your Christ Light is?

* What do you think God Space is?

* What does "There is nothing 'outside' now" mean to you?

* What difference could it make if you relax before you pray?

* What does it mean to connect with and open your Heart?

* How do you breathe through your Heart?

* What is a cleansing breath?

* What does it mean to stay in your Heart Space while you pray?

* Would it make a difference if you paused in the middle of breathing?

* How is Heart Centered Prayer different from other kinds of prayer?

Talk-able Topics ... Cool Conversations

* What do you feel an energy loop is?

* What is the Silence?

* Does it matter if you close your eyes when you pray? Why?

* Do you feel there is a difference between prayer and meditation?

* What could you do to ease your nerves about praying with others?

* What are some words you could use to begin and end group prayer?

* What are some words you could close a group prayer with?

* What do you think "you're WITHIN God already" means?

* What does "THE FEELING IN PRAYER IS WHAT MAKES IT ALL REAL", and why do you think it was capitalized?

* What is your God-Voice, and how is it different from your regular everyday voice (if you think it is)?

* What does, "It's not asking for things or to just get your way, it's letting the Voice of your Truth have its Say; Remembering you are more than the body you're in, taking time in the Silence to step out of the din.", mean to you?

* Will reading this book change anything about the way you pray? Why?

* If you could chat with the author, what would you like to say?

Trish Yancey has been a student of Unity and the principles of Truth since the age of six. She lives in sunny South Florida embraced by her husband, children and grandchildren, enfolded within the love of friends and family. Trish enjoys sharing Spiritual Truth as the Associate Spiritual Leader for Youth, Family & Education at Unity of the Palm Beaches, where she has served since 2006. She has also been bringing science to life for students of all ages for more than two decades through her educational company, Fun Learning Adventures. This book is from her Heart to yours, shared with Love, Light and Gratitude.

Coming soon … more books from the Heart designed to inspire and enlighten readers of all ages. Please stay attuned!

Find my books at www.TrishYancey.com, and please don't hesitate to email me any time at trish@TrishYancey.com if you would like to get in touch. I would love to hear from you!

Made in the USA
Columbia, SC
28 June 2017